A Message to Grown-Ups

This book is designed to be used anywhere and at any time. Dirty pages and bent corners are the mark of a true explorer (and a well-loved book). Toss it in your bag for outdoor adventures, point at the pictures during bedtime reading, or just hand it to your child and see what sparks their imagination.

As you explore together, encourage kiddos to use their senses. Ask questions like "What can you hear?" or "What do you see?" Share your own wonder too. Remember it's okay if they wander off in the middle of an activity to investigate something new. Science doesn't happen in a straight line, even for adults. Your child is learning to engage with the natural world. Let their curiosity lead the way and enjoy making memories that will last a lifetime.

Happy exploring,

Emily Greenhalgh

Hi, Bug Explorers!

Welcome to the crawling, buzzing, hopping world of bugs and their friends! Bugs come in all shapes and sizes, from tiny ants to moths as big as your head.

There are *way* more bugs than people in the world. You can find them almost anywhere! They live underground, way up in trees, under rocks, or inside logs. All bugs are important to life on Earth.

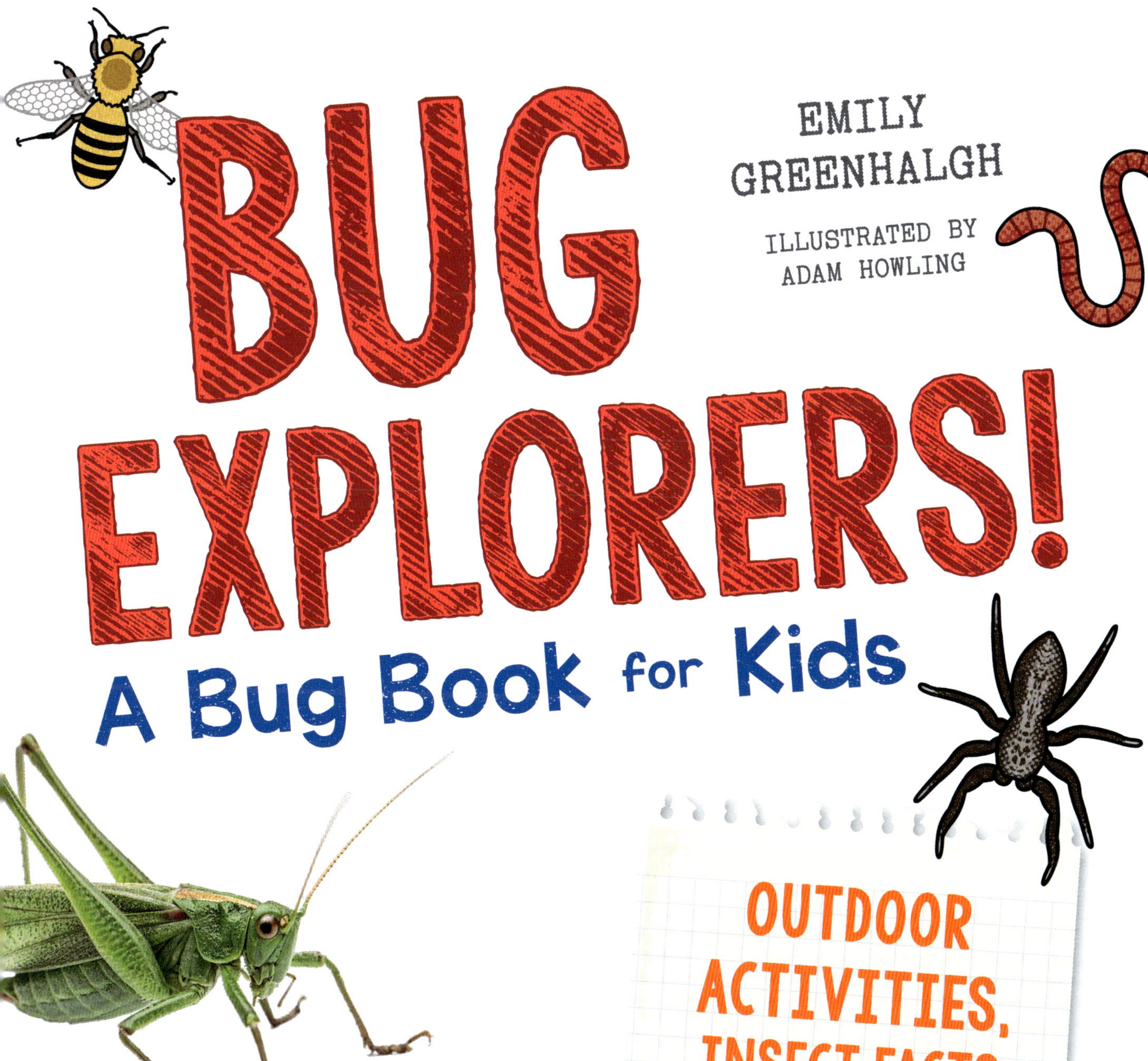

BUG EXPLORERS!

A Bug Book for Kids

EMILY GREENHALGH

ILLUSTRATED BY ADAM HOWLING

OUTDOOR ACTIVITIES, INSECT FACTS & STICKERS

Z KIDS • NEW YORK

To Dad, who was always ready to play outside

Z Kids
An imprint of Zeitgeist™
A division of Penguin Random House LLC
1745 Broadway, New York, NY 10019
zeitgeistpublishing.com
penguinrandomhouse.com

ISBN: 9798217151189
Ebook ISBN: 9798217151172

Printed in the United States of America
2nd Printing

Illustrations by Adam Howling
Photography © by Shutterstock.com and Getty Images
Book design by Katy Brown
Edited by Erin Nelson

The authorized representative in the EU for product safety and compliance is Penguin Random House Ireland, Morrison Chambers, 32 Nassau Street, Dublin D02 YH68, Ireland. https://eu-contact.penguin.ie

IS IT A BUG?

Lots of things can be a bug! Insects all have six legs. Some can fly (like butterflies) and others scurry or hop to move. Spiders have eight legs instead of six, centipedes have dozens of legs, and worms have no legs at all. You can find lots of bugs in the world if you keep your eyes peeled!

EXPLORER'S BACKPACK

To be a bug explorer, all you need is your curiosity and this book. But there are a few other things that might help you along the way!

A magnifying glass to see super-tiny bugs

Binoculars to see faraway bugs, especially in trees

A notebook and crayons to draw your new friends

A hat to shield you from the sun

Comfortable shoes that are okay to get dirty

Sunscreen to keep your skin safe

A water bottle for when you're thirsty

TIPS FOR BUG EXPLORERS

1. **Be brave.**
   Bugs are more scared of you than you are of them.

2. **Keep your eyes peeled.**
   Look up high and down low, too.

3. **Get dirty.**
   Carefully check under rocks, leaves, or piles of sticks.

4. **Use your ears.**
   Listen for buzzes, chirps, or the flutter of wings to help you find them.

5. **Look but don't touch.**
   Respect bugs' homes by not disturbing nests, webs, or bug hills.

BUG SAFETY

Always check in with your grown-up before approaching or touching a bug.

STICKERS

Keep your eyes peeled!

Use the stickers in the back of the book to mark when you complete an outdoor activity—or spot a bug!

BUG PROTECTOR PLEDGE

I promise
to be gentle and kind to all bugs
I meet in the world.

WRITE YOUR NAME HERE

Ants

There are red ants, black ants, and even ants that farm tiny mushrooms! Ants are superstrong and work as a team.

ANTHILL

WEAVER ANT

DID YOU KNOW?
Ants have two stomachs—one to feed themselves, and one to store food to share with their friends.

DID YOU KNOW?
Some ants can float together in water like a raft!

OUTDOOR ACTIVITY

Anthill Detective

CITY WALKS | BACKYARD EXPLORING | PARK PLAY | NATURE HIKES

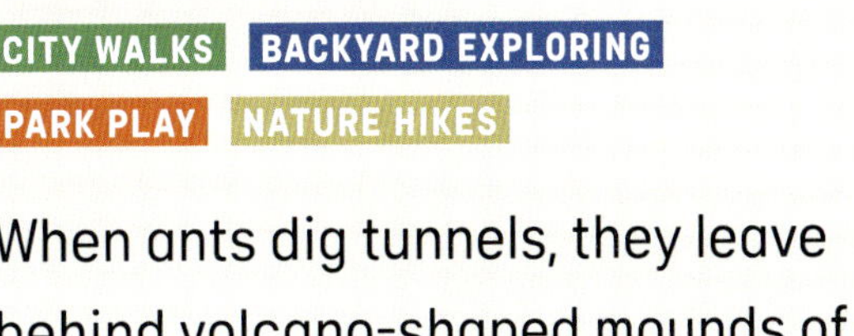

When ants dig tunnels, they leave behind volcano-shaped mounds of sand or dirt called anthills. Can you find one? Let ants lead the way! Ants travel in lines, following each other's smells.

1. If you see ants, follow their path to find their hill.
2. How many ants can you count? Try dropping two different types of food near the hill to lure them out.
3. Which crumbs do they like best?

Nature's Farmers

Leaf-cutter ants are tiny farmers with big jobs! These ants plant fungus gardens underground. They carry leaf pieces back to their home and use them to feed their garden. This fungus is their food, and ants take care of it every day. Just like human farmers!

LEAF-CUTTER ANT

OUTDOOR ACTIVITY

Be an Ant Farmer!

BACKYARD EXPLORING PARK PLAY
NATURE HIKES CAMPING

Collect already fallen leaves to bring back to your "farm." What type of fruit, grain, or vegetable would you like to grow? Let's pretend!

1. Once you have your leaf pile, break each one into tiny pieces. This is your mulch—food for your garden.
2. Spread your mulch onto the earth. Pretend to water it. Even though this garden won't grow, you're helping to break down leaves to give back to the Earth.

Walkingsticks

These bugs hide in plain sight. Walkingsticks live high in trees, where they blend in with the branches. This disguise helps keep them safe from animals that want to eat them. Walkingsticks move very slowly and munch on green leaves.

WALKINGSTICK

DID YOU KNOW?
The largest stick bug in the world is as long as a cat!

OUTDOOR ACTIVITY

Build Your Own Stick Bug

BACKYARD EXPLORING PARK PLAY NATURE HIKES CAMPING

Stick bugs are hard to spot, but you can build your own!

1. Find a long, thin stick for the body. Put it on the ground where you want to build your bug.
2. Gather six small sticks for the legs and two long sticks for your bug's antennae.
3. Find two black rocks for the bug's eyes.
4. Now put your stick bug together!

Camouflage

Some bugs are masters of disguise! Camouflage is when an animal's body can blend in with its surroundings. For bugs, this means looking like leaves, bark, dirt, or rocks.

COMMON GREEN SHIELDBUG

WOLF SPIDER

PEPPERED MOTH

OUTDOOR ACTIVITY

Now You See Me, Now You Don't!

BACKYARD EXPLORING PARK PLAY CAMPING

1. Pretend you're a bug trying to blend in with the environment around you.
2. Look around. What colors do you see? Brown leaves? Gray bark? Green grass?
3. Pick a spot and try to blend in. Can you find something to hide behind that matches the color of your clothes?
4. Ask your grown-up, "Can you spot me?" Then switch—they hide, you seek!

Pill Bugs

Pill bugs roll up into balls to hide their soft bellies. That's how they get the nickname "roly-poly."

PILL BUG

DID YOU KNOW?

Pill bugs shed their shells as they grow. This is called molting. If you find a pill bug that's half purple, that means it just molted!

OUTDOOR ACTIVITY

Pill Bug Practice

BACKYARD EXPLORING PARK PLAY

Can you be a pill bug?

1. Find a soft spot in the grass.
2. Crawl along the ground on your hands and knees.
3. Have your grown-up shout "BOO!" and then curl into a ball.
4. Can you stay in a ball shape for one . . . two . . . three seconds?!
5. How many roly-poly balls can you make?

Worms

Worms help keep our world full of life! Worm poop, called castings, is like superfood for plants. Thank you, worm poop!

DID YOU KNOW?
Earthworms breathe through their skin.

DID YOU KNOW?
If a worm gets hurt, it can regrow parts of its body!

EARTHWORM

OUTDOOR ACTIVITY

Worm Races

BACKYARD EXPLORING | CAMPING

Let's build a worm racetrack!

1. Gather four thick sticks to form a square on the ground.
2. Fill that square with some wet dirt.
3. Use more sticks, rocks, or your fingers to make paths in the dirt.
4. Next, loosen the soil around you to find your worms.
5. Gently pick them up—don't squeeze! Put the worms in your racetrack and watch what happens. Which worm wriggles first? Do any of them make it to the end?
6. Make sure you put your worms back where you found them when you're done.

Millipedes

Millipedes have lots and *lots* of little legs. Their bodies are made of hard pieces that fit together like a puzzle. They're usually brown or black, but can be orange, red, or purple, too.

DID YOU KNOW?
Millipedes have an exoskeleton—a skeleton on the outside.

AMERICAN GIANT MILLIPEDE

DID YOU KNOW?
The motyxia millipede glows blue in the dark!

MOTYXIA MILLIPEDE

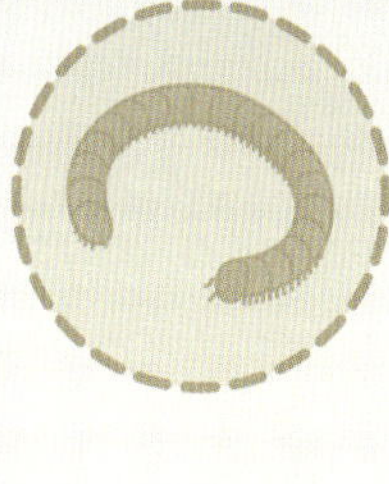

OUTDOOR ACTIVITY

Millipede House Hunt

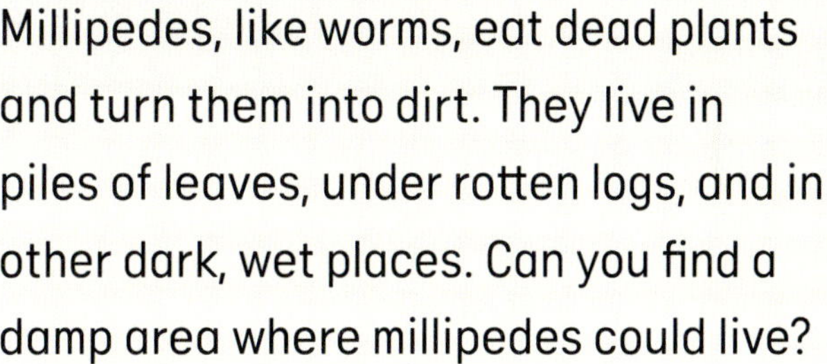

CAMPING PARK PLAY NATURE HIKES BACKYARD EXPLORING

Millipedes, like worms, eat dead plants and turn them into dirt. They live in piles of leaves, under rotten logs, and in other dark, wet places. Can you find a damp area where millipedes could live?

1. Gently turn over rocks or logs and see if you can spot any.
2. How many legs can you count before they scurry away?
3. Did you see any other wriggly bugs?

Spiders

Spiders have eight legs, two round body parts, and fangs for eating bugs. Most make silk from their bodies to spin webs—kind of like magic string! They live all over the world and look very different because they need different features to survive.

SAFETY

Some spiders are dangerous. If you see a black spider with a red marking, like the female black widow, tell a grown-up and stay far away.

DID YOU KNOW?

By catching bugs in their webs, spiders help our ecosystem stay balanced.

BLACK WIDOW

TARANTULA

DID YOU KNOW?

Tarantulas are covered in sharp, tiny hairs they flick at predators when they're scared!

OUTDOOR ACTIVITY

Spiderweb Search

BACKYARD EXPLORING CITY WALKS PARK PLAY CAMPING

Spiderwebs are sticky traps spiders make to catch bugs to eat. Some are round like a wheel, and some are messy and hidden, but all help spiders get their dinner.

1. On your next walk or outdoor adventure, see if you can find different web types.
2. Can you find one of each type of web? Do you spot any spiders in their web?

Venom

Venom is a kind of poison that some animals use to protect themselves or catch food. They can put venom into another animal with a bite or a sting.

FIRE ANTS

SAFETY

You should stay away from venomous bugs. They like to be left alone.

BUCK MOTH CATERPILLAR

DID YOU KNOW?
A venom attack makes animals feel sick or sleepy.

BROWN RECLUSE SPIDER

OUTDOOR ACTIVITY

Move Like a Venomous Bug

BACKYARD EXPLORING CITY WALKS

PARK PLAY CAMPING

Let's be venomous bugs!

Shhh . . . you're a tiny creature with a big secret: You have venom to protect you—but you never want to use it!

1. Find a quiet spot by a bush, rock, or tree.
2. Crouch and be still. What do you see? Any tiny bugs moving?
3. Now crawl slowly. Are you a spider? An ant? A scorpion?

Scorpions

During the day, scorpions hide under rocks or logs. At night, they come out looking for tasty bugs to eat. Scorpions use a venomous barb at the end of their tail to sting. Baby scorpions are called scorplings!

SAFETY

Scorpions are very dangerous. If you see one, stay away and tell a grown-up!

ARIZONA BARK SCORPION

DID YOU KNOW?
Scorpions glow bright green under a special type of light called a black light.

Buggy Bingo!

BACKYARD EXPLORING | PARK PLAY | CAMPING | NATURE HIKES | CITY WALKS

Can you find enough things to make a line on this bingo card? Don't forget to look close to the ground and up in the sky!

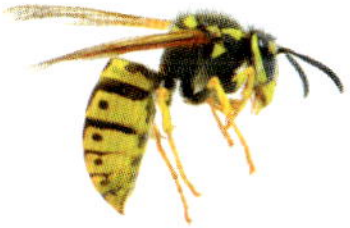 SOMETHING YELLOW	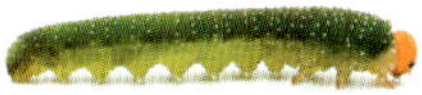 SOMETHING THAT CRAWLS	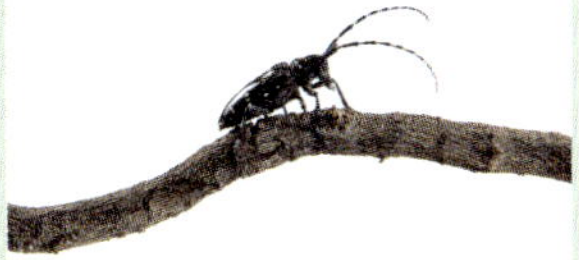 A BUG ON A TREE	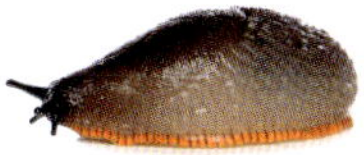 SOMETHING SLIMY
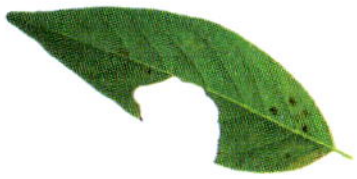 BITE MARKS ON A LEAF	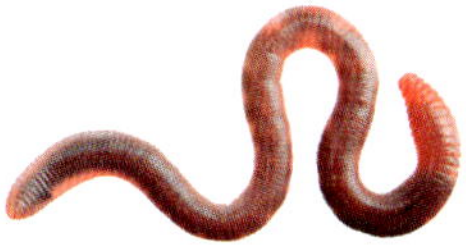 SOMETHING THAT WIGGLES	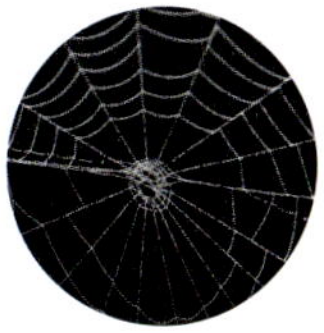 A WEB	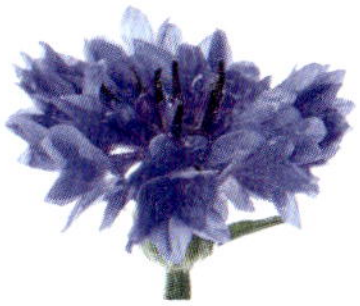 SOMETHING BLUE
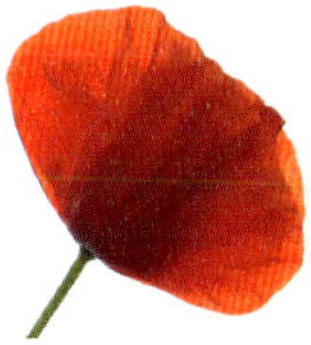 SOMETHING ORANGE	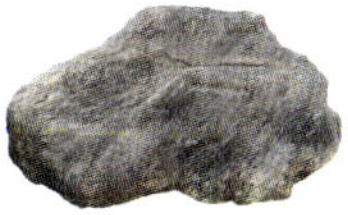 A BIG ROCK	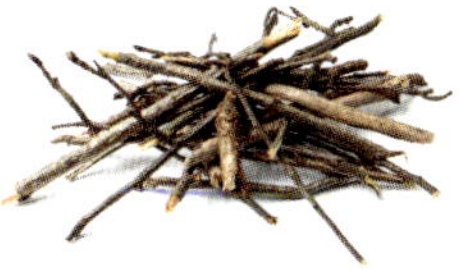 A PILE OF STICKS	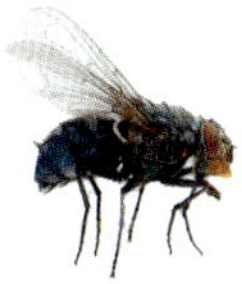 SOMETHING WITH WINGS
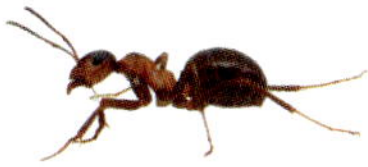 AN ANTHILL OR TRAIL OF ANTS	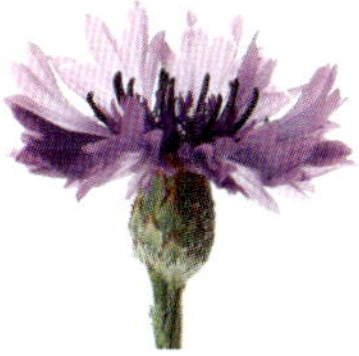 SOMETHING PURPLE	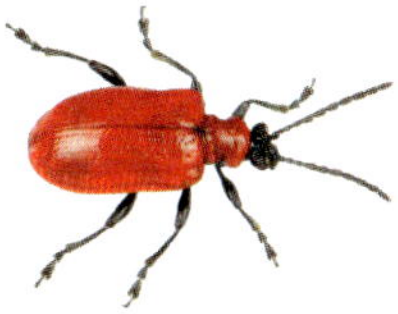 SOMETHING RED	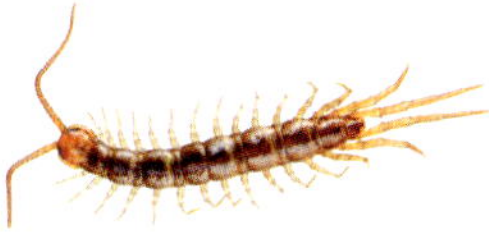 SOMETHING WITH LOTS OF LEGS

Dragonflies

Dragonflies are colorful bugs with long, see-through wings. Their wing shape makes them great at flying. They can fly in six directions: up, down, forward, back, and side to side. They can even hover in place, like a helicopter!

BLUE DASHER DRAGONFLY

DID YOU KNOW?
The globe skimmer dragonfly can fly across the ocean without stopping to rest.

OUTDOOR ACTIVITY

Dragonfly Spotter

PARK PLAY NATURE HIKES CAMPING

Dragonflies live near water, like ponds, lakes, and rivers. Stay with your grown-up as you become a dragonfly spotter!

1. Find plants, rocks, or sticks near the water where dragonflies might rest, and listen for buzzing!
2. Hold your hands up to your eyes, like binoculars. (Or grab your binoculars, if you have them on you.) Can you see anything?
3. What other flying bugs do you spot?

Butterflies

Our butterfly friends flutter from flower to flower, sipping sweet nectar and spreading pollen. Some butterflies fly very far—over entire deserts and oceans—to get warm when it's cold.

GIANT SWALLOWTAIL BUTTERFLY

DID YOU KNOW?

Butterflies taste with their feet!

OUTDOOR ACTIVITY

Bathtime for Bugs

BACKYARD EXPLORING **PARK PLAY** **CAMPING**

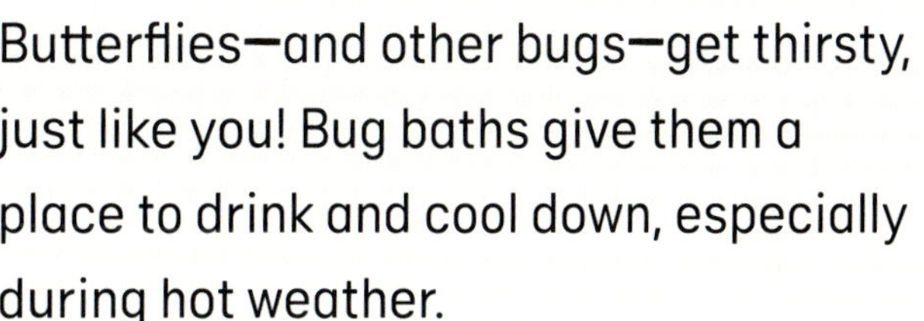

Butterflies—and other bugs—get thirsty, just like you! Bug baths give them a place to drink and cool down, especially during hot weather.

1. Ask your grown-up for a small dish and some water.
2. Put your dish in the shade near flowers you think bugs might like.
3. Find enough smooth rocks to fill up your dish. This makes a safe landing area for the bugs.
4. Now add water and watch for bugs! How many different kinds can you see?

Metamorphosis

Some bugs don't stay the same—they completely change as they grow! That big change is called metamorphosis. Butterflies and moths both start out as an egg, become a wiggly caterpillar, then wrap into a chrysalis or cocoon . . . and come out with new wings!

1. EGGS

DID YOU KNOW?

Beetles, moths, and flies go through their own metamorphosis, too!

POLYPHEMUS MOTH

3. CHRYSALIS

2. CATERPILLAR
4. BUTTERFLY!

OUTDOOR ACTIVITY

Change in Action

BACKYARD EXPLORING PARK PLAY NATURE HIKES CAMPING CITY WALKS

Take a minute to notice some changes around you. Can you spot any signs of metamorphosis?

1. Look closely at leaves or twigs: Do you see a curled leaf, a hanging shape, or a tiny case? It might be a chrysalis or cocoon!
2. Check on plants or stems: Are there caterpillars crawling or munching?
3. Look in the sky or on flowers: Do you see butterflies or moths fluttering around?

Moths

Moths are fuzzy nighttime cousins of butterflies. They are often drawn to light. This might be because they use the moon and stars to find their way.

DID YOU KNOW?

Most moths are nocturnal, which means they sleep during the day and fly at night.

LUNA MOTH

OUTDOOR ACTIVITY

Moth Spotlight

BACKYARD EXPLORING | CAMPING

Be the moth's light!

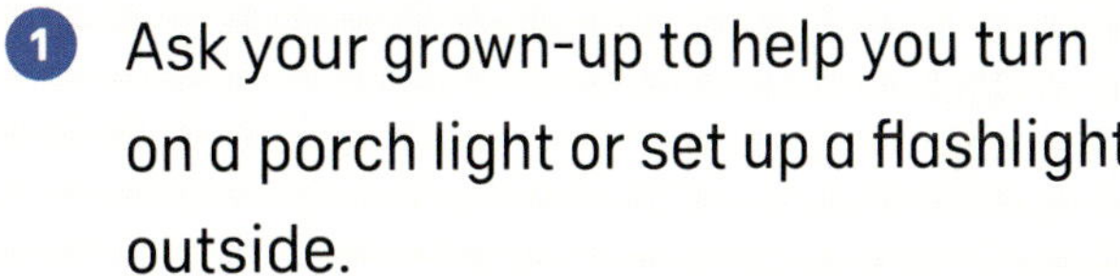

1. Ask your grown-up to help you turn on a porch light or set up a flashlight outside.
2. Watch closely. How many moths do you see? Do they look the same or different?
3. Make sure to turn off your light when you're done—and watch the moths flutter away.

Pollinators

Some bugs have a superpower—they help plants grow! When they fly or crawl from flower to flower, they move pollen—the golden dust flowers need to grow fruit and new flowers. This is called pollination. Bees, butterflies, beetles, and even ants can be pollinators!

HONEYBEE

MONARCH BUTTERFLY

OUTDOOR ACTIVITY

Pollinator Detective!

BACKYARD EXPLORING CITY WALKS
PARK PLAY CAMPING

1. Find a flower—any color, any size. Look closely . . . is anyone visiting it?
2. Listen: Do you hear buzzing?
3. Wait and watch. Can you spot a bee, butterfly, beetle, or ant?
4. Gently follow the bug with your eyes (not your hands!) to see where it goes next.

Bumblebees

Bumblebees are fuzzy fliers with yellow and black stripes. Their furry bodies make them great pollinators—dust gets stuck on their fur! Listen closely. Bumblebees *buzz* loudly when they fly.

DID YOU KNOW?
Only female bumblebees have stingers.

AMERICAN BUMBLEBEE

SAFETY
Keep clear of bumblebees' nests!

DID YOU KNOW?
Aww—sometimes bumblebees take naps in flowers!

OUTDOOR ACTIVITY

Bumblebee Bouquet

BACKYARD EXPLORING

PARK PLAY CITY WALKS

How many different colored flowers can you find? Check them off as you go! And keep a lookout for bees.

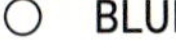

○ BLUE

○ PINK

○ PURPLE

○ YELLOW

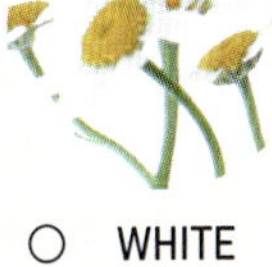

○ WHITE

Honeybees

Honeybees have a special part of their tummy called a honey stomach where they store nectar from flowers to turn into honey! When worker bees get back to their hive, they barf up the nectar to share it with their friends. Teamwork!

DID YOU KNOW?

There are three types of honeybees in each hive—the queen, workers, and drones.

SAFETY

Ouch! It can hurt to be stung by a honeybee. The best way to avoid a bee sting is to hold very still.

DID YOU KNOW?

Honeybees have five eyes, but none of those eyes can see red!

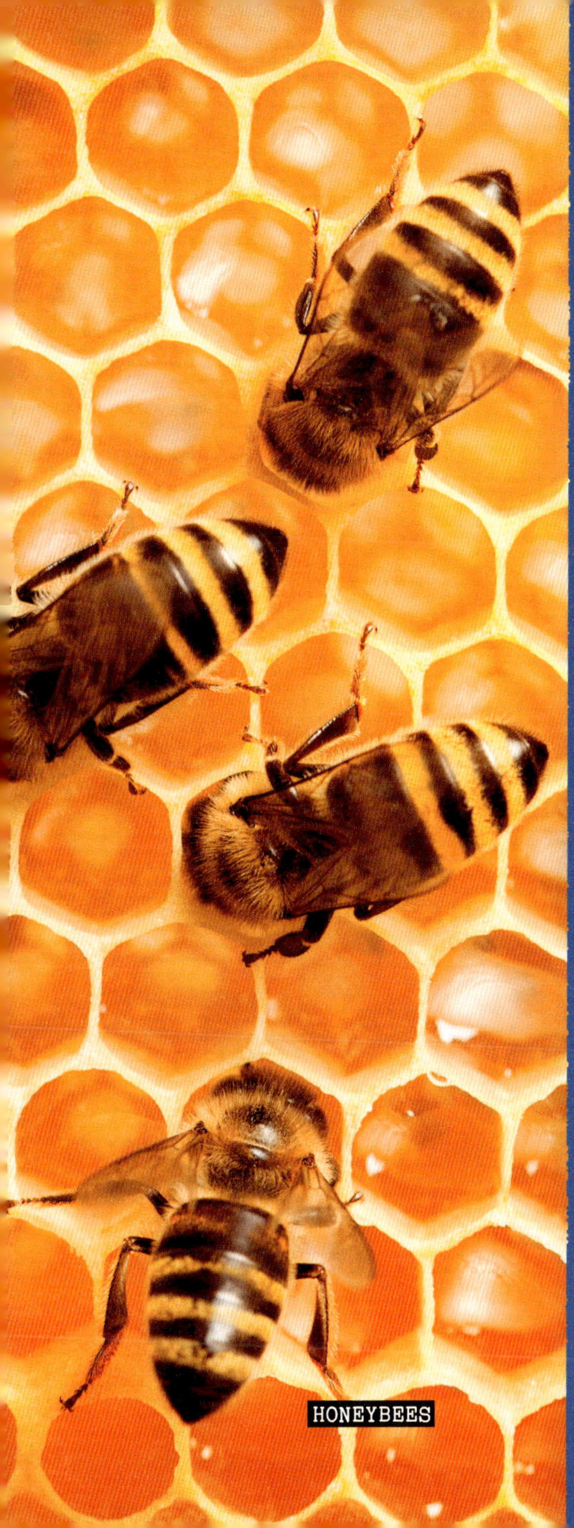

OUTDOOR ACTIVITY

Waggle Dance

Honeybees talk to each other through dance. By waggling their bottoms and moving different ways, honeybees tell each other things like how to find flowers with lots of pollen or where the closest water is. Can you come up with your own waggle dance?

1. Waggle your bottom while walking a few steps.
2. Circle back around to the start.
3. Ask your grown-up to do their silliest waggle dance, too!

HONEYBEES

Wasps

Wasps are flying bugs with shiny bodies and strong stingers. Some, like yellowjackets, live in big families and build papery nests, but others like to live alone—they're called solitary wasps. Watch your step! Some wasps build their home underground.

SAFETY

While honeybees can only sting once, wasps can sting many times because their stinger doesn't get stuck. If you see a wasp, tell a grown-up and give it plenty of space.

MUD DAUBER WASP

DID YOU KNOW?
Some wasps sing with a buzzy noise when they're building their home!

OUTDOOR ACTIVITY

Wing Watcher

BACKYARD EXPLORING | PARK PLAY | NATURE HIKES | CAMPING | CITY WALKS

How many winged critters can you find in this mini scavenger hunt? Check them off as you go!

○ BUTTERFLY

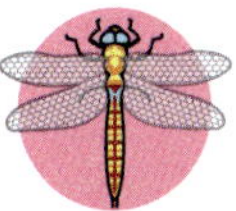

○ DRAGONFLY

○ BEETLE

○ MOTH

○ LADYBUG

○ BUMBLEBEE

○ HONEYBEE

○ WASP

Fireflies

Fireflies use the lower part of their belly, called a lantern, to glow in the dark. The lantern helps them talk to other fireflies and warn predators that they taste bad. Some large groups of fireflies can flash all at once!

DID YOU KNOW?
Fireflies aren't really flies—they're a type of beetle!

BIG DIPPER FIREFLY

DID YOU KNOW?
Each kind of firefly flashes in its own special pattern—like a secret light dance!

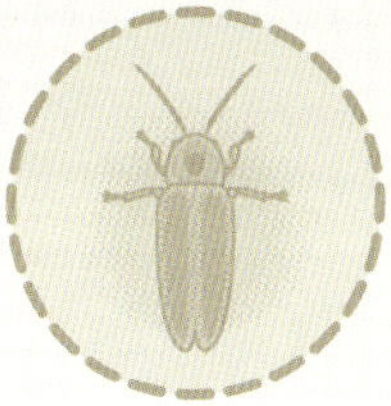

OUTDOOR ACTIVITY

Flashlight Talks

BACKYARD EXPLORING | CAMPING

Use light to talk to each other like fireflies do!

1. Find a flashlight and head outside with your grown-up. (This works best when it's dark.)
2. Hold up your flashlight and put your hand over it to cover the light.
3. Move your hand away to flash the light. How many letters are in your name? Can you do one flash for each letter?

Bug Senses

Bugs don't use their senses the same way we do. Ants smell with their antennae. Butterflies taste with their feet! Spiders feel tiny movements through the ground and their webs. Many bugs have big eyes that can see in lots of directions at once.

COMMON BLUE DAMSELFLY

OUTDOOR ACTIVITY

Sharpen Your Bug Senses!

BACKYARD EXPLORING PARK PLAY
CAMPING NATURE HIKES

Let's explore like bugs do.

1. Crawl low like a spider. What do you *feel* under your hands and feet? (Dirt? Rocks? Roots?)
2. Close your eyes and *listen*: Can you hear buzzing? Rustling leaves?
3. Sniff the air like an ant. What do you *smell*?
4. *Touch* a leaf or bark gently. Is it bumpy, smooth, soft, or scratchy?

Ladybugs

Ladybugs are usually red with black spots, but some ladybugs have stripes—or no markings at all. They can be orange or yellow too! Ladybugs' colors tell predators, "Don't eat me, I taste bad!"

SEVEN-SPOTTED LADYBIRD

DID YOU KNOW?
Some people say it's good luck if a ladybug lands on you!

OUTDOOR ACTIVITY

Spot the Spots

BACKYARD EXPLORING CITY WALKS PARK PLAY NATURE HIKES CAMPING

Can you find any bugs with spots?

1. Get close to flowers and bushes.
2. Look up in trees and down in the grass.
3. Circle a dot (or smudge with dirt!) for every spotted bug you see!

More Beetles!

DID YOU KNOW?

Almost half of all the insects in the world are beetles! There are beetles in every color of the rainbow.

OUTDOOR ACTIVITY

Rainbow Safari

BACKYARD EXPLORING | CITY WALKS | PARK PLAY | NATURE HIKES

Some animals use bright colors to scare off predators. But they can also use their colors to blend in. Try to find one bug for each color of the rainbow.

- ○ RED
- ○ ORANGE
- ○ YELLOW
- ○ GREEN
- ○ BLUE
- ○ INDIGO
- ○ VIOLET

SAFETY

Ouch! Some beetles bite. Always check with a grown-up before getting too close.

June Bugs

June bugs are small beetles with hairy bellies. They make a loud buzzing noise when they fly. They're clumsy flyers, though. They sometimes bump into walls, windows, and even people. Don't worry, they don't bite!

GREEN JUNE BEETLE

DID YOU KNOW?
June bug babies sleep under the dirt for two or three years before they come to the surface as adults!

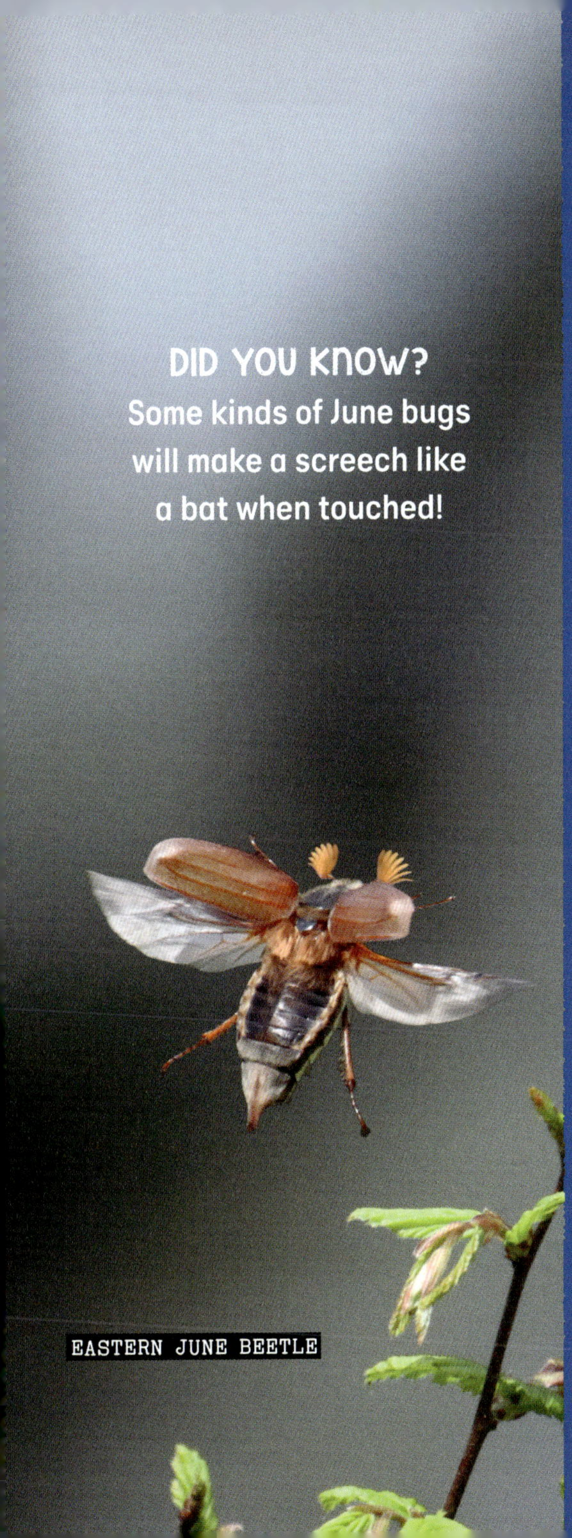

DID YOU KNOW?
Some kinds of June bugs will make a screech like a bat when touched!

EASTERN JUNE BEETLE

OUTDOOR ACTIVITY

Dizzy Fliers

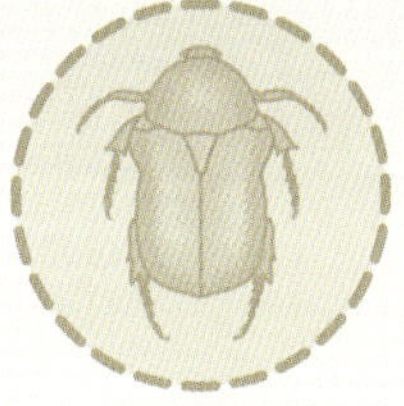

BACKYARD EXPLORING PARK PLAY NATURE HIKES

Pretend to be a silly flier!

1. Spin around in a circle, then try to walk in a straight line. Do you fall over and bump into things too? Look out for rocks and bushes!
2. When you get tired, lie down in the grass and look up at the sky. Do you see any flying bugs? What do you hear?

Cicadas

Have you ever heard the trees buzz in summer? That's probably cicadas. Cicadas are the loudest insect in the world. They can be as loud as a lawn mower!

PHARAOH CICADA

DID YOU KNOW?
Cicadas *buzzzzzz* by vibrating their bodies.

OUTDOOR ACTIVITY

Cicada Chats

BACKYARD EXPLORING PARK PLAY

Can you talk like a cicada?

1. Cup your hands over your mouth and make a buzzing noise.
2. Try to say your name with your mouth still covered. How far away can you move from your grown-up and have them still understand what you're saying?
3. Practice your loud buzz, but don't go too far!

Grasshoppers

Grasshoppers' long back legs make them excellent jumpers! They rub their back legs on their wings to make chirping and buzzing sounds. This is how they talk to each other!

RED-LEGGED GRASSHOPPER

DID YOU KNOW?
When grasshoppers are scared, they spit to protect themselves!

OUTDOOR ACTIVITY

Grasshopper Hide-and-Seek

BACKYARD EXPLORING | PARK PLAY

1. Find a patch of tall grass to look for grasshopper friends. They like sunshine, so head to a sunny spot.
2. They'll be on a plant, not on the ground. So check on leaves, stems, and flowers.
3. Do you spot any other jumping bugs? What else do you see in the grass?

Crickets

Male crickets make loud chirping noises, especially at night. They do it by rubbing their wings together. Listen closely in the summer—crickets chirp faster when it's warm out!

DID YOU KNOW?
A cricket's ears are by its knees!

FIELD CRICKET

OUTDOOR ACTIVITY

Cricket Chorus

BACKYARD EXPLORING | CAMPING | PARK PLAY

1. Anytime it's dark out, close your eyes and listen for crickets.
2. Point in the direction of the chirping.
3. If you're outside, what happens when you walk toward it?
4. Did the sound get louder? That means you're going the right way!

OUTDOOR ACTIVITY

I Spy ABCs

BACKYARD EXPLORING | PARK PLAY | CAMPING | CITY WALKS | NATURE HIKES

From A to Z, there's so much to see! Can you find something for every letter in the alphabet? Try to cross off the boxes that spell your name.

m
MUSHROOMS
n
NEST
o
ORANGE FLOWERS
p
PINE CONE
Q
QUIET BUG
R
ROUND BUG
S
SPOTTED BUG
T
TALL TREES
U
UNDERGROUND BUG
V
VERY TALL GRASS
W
WINGED BUG
X
EXOSKELETON
Y
YELLOW BUG
Z
ZEBRA-STRIPED BUG

Praying Mantises

When praying mantises feel in danger, they get as big as they can. They stand up tall and spread their arms and wings wide! This scares away animals that might want to eat them.

EUROPEAN MANTIS

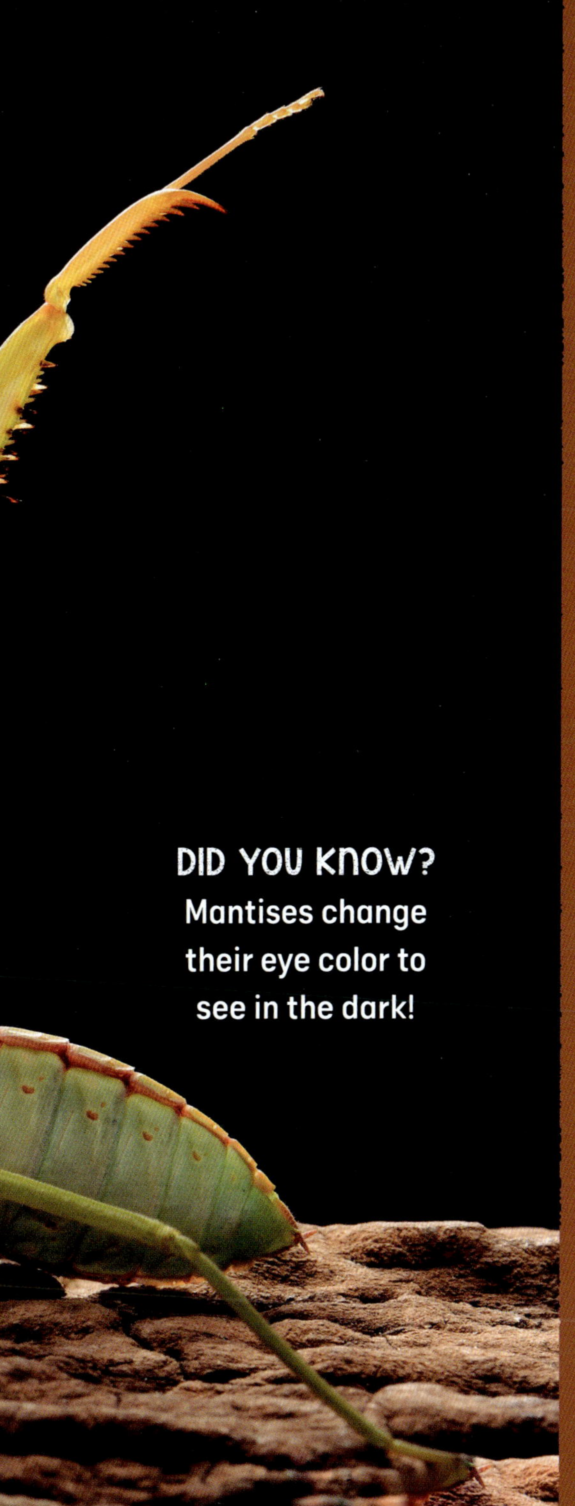

DID YOU KNOW?
Mantises change their eye color to see in the dark!

OUTDOOR ACTIVITY

Patient as a Praying Mantis

BACKYARD EXPLORING | PARK PLAY | CAMPING

Mantises are "sit-and-wait" hunters. That means they sit very, ***very*** still and move only their heads back and forth to look for bugs to eat.

1. Find a comfortable spot near some trees, flowers, or long grass and sit very still.
2. Move only your head to look for bugs.
3. Do they crawl on the ground, wiggle in the dirt, or fly in the air?

Katydids

Katydids have amazing camouflage. They look just like a leaf! Katydids usually hide in trees and bushes.

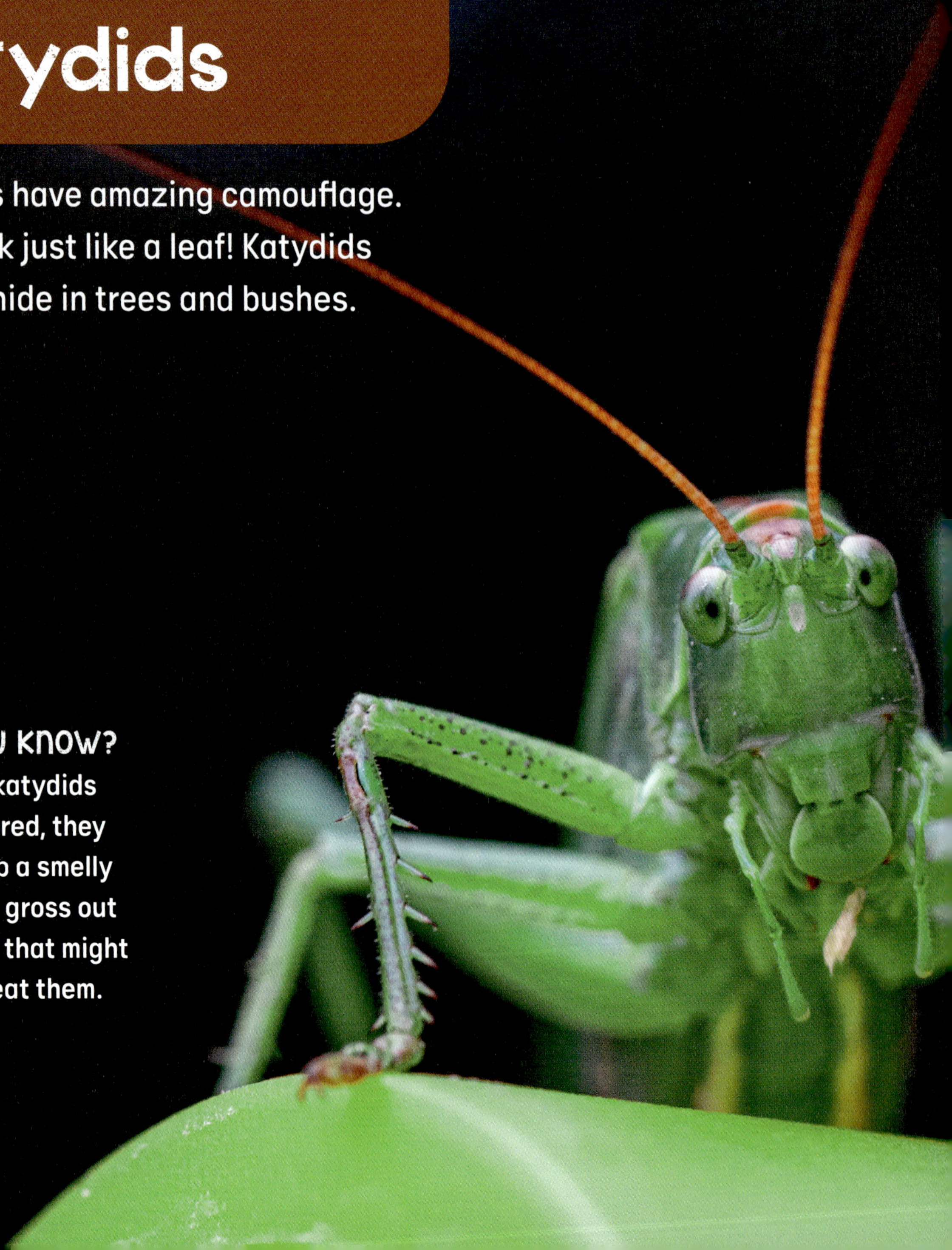

DID YOU KNOW?
When katydids get scared, they throw up a smelly liquid to gross out anything that might try to eat them.

KATYDID

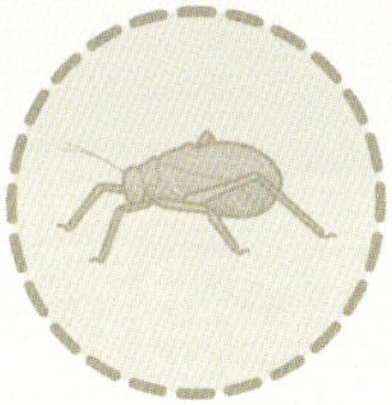

OUTDOOR ACTIVITY

Katydid Camouflage

BACKYARD EXPLORING PARK PLAY NATURE HIKES CAMPING

1. Look around for green leaves that look like katydids—round on one side and pointy on the other.
2. Gently turn them over.
3. Do you see signs of other bugs, like bite marks or eggs?

Hibernation

When it gets chilly, many bugs slow down or go to sleep—just like bears! Ladybugs cuddle in big groups. Honeybees shake together to keep warm. Earthworms curl up underground. This long winter rest is called hibernation.

OUTDOOR ACTIVITY

Bug Hotel!

BACKYARD EXPLORING PARK PLAY NATURE HIKES CAMPING

Bugs need a place to rest or sleep, especially during the winter. Let's build them a bug hotel!

1. Collect treasures like small logs, large sticks, and pieces of rotting wood or bark.
2. Pile them up in a damp, shady area outside.
3. Then stuff some dead leaves, small rocks, pine cones, and pine needles into the pile. Your bug friends thank you!

Springtails

Springtails are teeny, tiny bugs. They are only as big as the tip of a pen! They have a V-shaped "tail" under their bottom that helps them jump super high! Their jumps are designed for quick escapes.

WHITE SPRINGTAILS

DID YOU KNOW?
You can find springtails in damp places like soil, moss, or rotten logs.

SLENDER SPRINGTAIL

OUTDOOR ACTIVITY

Invent-a-Bug

BACKYARD EXPLORING | PARK PLAY | CAMPING

You've learned so much about bugs! If you could be any bug, what would you be? Why don't you invent your own?

1. How many legs would you have?
2. Would you jump, hop, crawl, or fly?
3. What color would you be?
4. Where would you make your home?

Pretend to be your cool new bug.
Great work!

Leafhoppers

Leafhoppers are tiny bugs that can jump and fly. They're even smaller than a grain of rice! Leafhoppers are found wherever plants grow. Some are plain, but others are brightly colored or have stripes!

LEAFHOPPER

GREEN LEAFHOPPERS

DID YOU KNOW?
Leafhoppers leave behind a sweet sap called honeydew that other bugs love to eat.

OUTDOOR ACTIVITY

Leafhopper Hunt

BACKYARD EXPLORING | PARK PLAY | CAMPING | NATURE HIKES | CITY WALKS

Let's go on a leaf hunt! Sometimes when leafhoppers eat a lot, they make leaf edges dry and brown.

1. Lean close to the ground and look for leaves that are dry and crispy.
2. Gently turn them over.
3. Look closely at the back. Can you spot any leafhoppers? (They can be hard to spot!)

Spittlebugs

As babies, spittlebugs hide in bubbles of foam to stay safe. That foam is called "spittle" and is how they get their name.

SPITTLEBUG FOAM

MEADOW SPITTLEBUG

OUTDOOR ACTIVITY

Spittlebug Sports

BACKYARD EXPLORING PARK PLAY

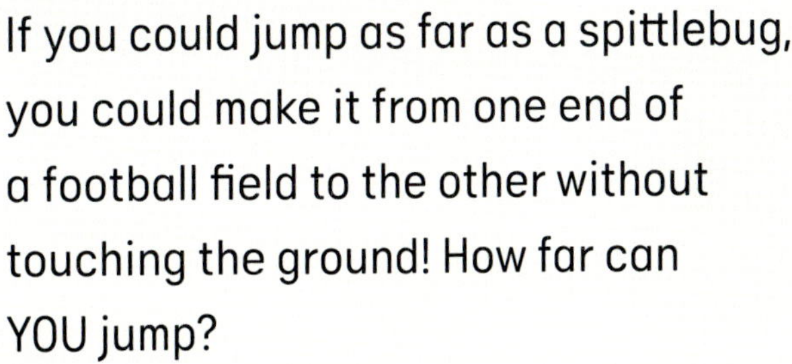

If you could jump as far as a spittlebug, you could make it from one end of a football field to the other without touching the ground! How far can YOU jump?

1. Find an even patch of ground and jump as FAR as you can.
2. Mark where you land with a rock, leaf, or stick.
3. Can you jump even farther the next time?

DID YOU KNOW?
Spittlebugs are known for their great hopping ability—like a frog!

Treehoppers

Treehoppers' horn-shaped bodies help them blend in with thorny leaves and plants. Some treehoppers shake their bodies to send messages to each other through the tree branches.

OAK TREEHOPPER

DID YOU KNOW?
Some treehoppers make friends with local ants. The ants protect the baby treehoppers and get tasty honeydew to eat in return.

OAK TREEHOPPER BABIES

OUTDOOR ACTIVITY

Shake, Shake, Shake!

BACKYARD EXPLORING | PARK PLAY | CAMPING

Can you communicate like a treehopper?

1. Find a big stick and hold one end while your grown-up holds the other.
2. *Shake, shake, shake!*
3. What story are you trying to tell with your shakes?

Draw What You See!

Bug scientists are called entomologists. They record what they see outside with drawings, photographs, and notes.

Emily Greenhalgh is a full-time science communicator and author of *Fun with Oceans and Seas* and *Fun with Outer Space*. Even as a kid, she never met a science fact she didn't like. She grew up in Rhode Island, staring into tide pools, flipping over logs to look at bugs, and counting shooting stars in the sky. Now she helps scientists tell their stories. In her spare time, she writes speculative fiction, does pottery, and enjoys putting cheese on things. She lives on Cape Cod, Massachusetts, with her husband, their two dogs, and one cat. Parents, you can find Emily online at emilygreenhalgh.com.

EXPLORE MORE COOL FACTS WITH THIS BUG-TASTIC COLORING BOOK!

BUG BOOK FOR KIDS

Coloring Fun and Awesome Facts

by Katie Henries-Meisner

Meet 25 weird and wonderful backyard bugs! This learn-through-coloring book provides kids with hours of screen-free coloring fun and teaches them exciting facts about these creepy-crawly creatures at the same time.

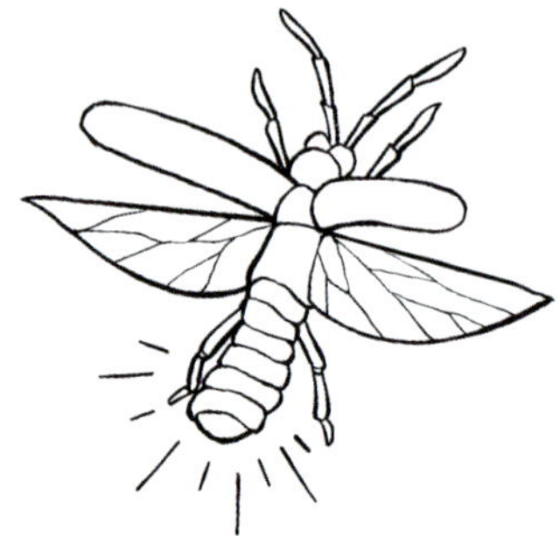